To Marie,

See you here then!

A

'85

GW01066222

Lake District Landscapes

JO DARKE

Lake District Landscapes

B T Batsford Ltd · London

©Opus Books 1983
First published 1983

ISBN 0 7134 4185 2

Typeset by Typewise Limited, Wembley
and printed in Hong Kong

Produced in co-operation with
Opus Books and published by
B. T. Batsford Ltd
4 Fitzhardinge Street
London W1H 0AH

CONTENTS

LIST OF ILLUSTRATIONS

Introduction

England's mountains and lakes lie between Morecambe Bay and the Solway Firth, deep broad estuary sands that bite into the land, isolating the platform on which the Lake District was formed. The Irish Sea makes a westward boundary and the Pennine range walls in the eastern side. Thus isolated in the extreme north-west corner of England the lakes over the centuries have built their singular charm, and in this man has collaborated with nature, engraving his signature on the rock and adding a final touch to the stirring beauty of mountain and lake. The signature, which to us may seem old, is fresh and new in comparison with the rock which as England's only mountain system rises like an irregularly shaped sandcastle that has been turned out of a more or less circular mould. This rocky dome was thrown up and altered by successive earth movements over many millions of years, ground down by wind and rain and finally subjected to a series of glaciations that scoured long narrow slits, some straight and some serpentine, into what remained of the dome. The glaciers moved from near the centre to the dome's outer edges, scooping out the lake and valley floors in a roughly radial pattern which, shown on a map, has been likened to the spokes of a wheel but is perhaps more reminiscent of a starfish stranded on stony ground.

Generally there are three types of stone in Lakeland, and this accounts for the sudden changes in mood or scene which attend the length of a lake like Ullswater and can be taken in at a glance from the summits of the hills. The rocks have been formed at varying periods and millions of years later they are stabilised, broadly speaking, in three north-westerly bands across the dome: in the south the low gentle hills of the Silurian rocks, in the centre the wild and jagged rocks of the volcanic series, and in the north the weighty shapes of the Skiddaw slates whose high mountains, unlike those in the volcanic band, have responded to the smoothing and rounding effects of wind and rain. Thus within this small and isolated region, little more than 30 miles across, the scenery can vary from the savage to the serene.

Into this land of water and rock man came: successive prehistoric tribes had settled, and had been overtaken by the warlike Brigantes by the time the Romans arrived. The Romans contained the Brigantes by encircling the region with garrisoned forts and by establishing a simple but effective system of roads at altitudes that prove a challenge to road builders and motor vehicles still. The Lake District was occupied by the Welsh-speaking Brigantes throughout the Roman administration, but by the late seventh century the fertile lowlands along the periphery of the lakes had been colonised by Angles coming overland from eastern England, and a century later the Norsemen came threading through the narrow valleys to find, amid the mountains and lakes, a land like their own. They cleared the woodlands to make settlements in the dales, and it is thought that they absorbed rather than vanquished the Celts, who by then had become 'Romanised' to a certain extent, and more used to the idea of coexisting with others. It is in the era of Norse settlement that the present culture and language of the lakes are thought to have their origins.

Today's distinctive landscape of long low farmsteads, and pastures contained by stone walls, was in many respects still quite new when

Overleaf Summer on Derwent Water. St Herbert's Island slumbers in solitude beneath the Derwent Fells: Cat Bells, Bowling End, Causey Pike and Barrow.

7

the lakes were 'discovered' late in the eighteenth century – for it was not until after Union with Scotland that the Border lands were able to settle down to a peaceful existence after centuries as disputed territory. As part of Scotland, Cumbria was taken for England by Henry II in 1157 but suffered terribly in raids by the Scottish heroes William Wallace and Robert Bruce. Thereafter Border families carried out savage raids on each other and each other's land. Union in 1603 eventually put an end to feuding, reiving and bloodshed; with the new stability quarries and mines were opened and communications improved. Fragile timber-framed dwellings gave way to stone houses built from material that was closest at hand, whether it was limestone, sandstone, granite or slate. The first tourists came upon a country that had changed relatively little over the intervening centuries, a country of hill farmers whose hardy sheep, chiefly of the

Herdwick breed, can survive on the exposed fells for most of the year. Today's farmers will be descendants of the 'statesmen,' or estates men, who held tenure of their farm buildings, land and sheep as a complete unit which was passed on entire to the next tenant. The glacial valleys with their round floors and lofty walls are isolated from their neighbours in the next dale, and market towns like Ambleside and Keswick have grown at the heads of the valleys, near the lakes, where there can be a measure of communication from dale to dale. The great mountains tower over the dales and their lakes, the slopes either rising immediately from water or pasture, or ranged along the horizon beyond the lower fells. Some mountains are steep, bleak and bare, some rounded and softened with grasses, and alight with heather in the summer or bracken in the autumn. Lakes like Windermere in the milder Silurian hills, or Ullswater snaking from volcanic

rock to Skiddaw slate, are fringed with woodlands of oak and ash and beech. By global standards the mountains are small, while more rain falls in this region than any other in rainy England – but the soft clarity of the air and the proportions of mountains and lakes create a true majesty. Ravens croak and hang around the cliff faces and kestrels or buzzards flutter and swoop; wildfowl bob on the water and herons, swans or even cormorants add their unmistakable, angular shapes to the scene. Red deer roam the southern fells and the shy, fleet roe deer can be glimpsed, while red squirrels survive in the mixed woodlands. The lakes teem with trout and coarse fish and they harbour their own species, like the char which swims in Windermere and some other lakes, and the rare schelly which is found in Ullswater, Red Tarn and Haweswater.

At first the wild mountains caused alarm, and early writers viewed them from a distance, and used words like 'fearful' and 'horrid'; the Victorians braved the scenery from their carriages following prescribed routes, ascending to easily-accessible and well-known view-points such as Jenkyn's Crag, known as 'Stations,' where they viewed the scene with the aid of a reducing, or 'Claude' glass. By then the poets had adopted the lakes and by so doing created an interest in their own lives and work as well as in the unforgettable landscapes about which they wrote. They evoked the notion of 'Lakeland' and unknowingly anticipated Britain's administrative reorganisation of 1974 which lumped together the former counties of Westmorland and Cumberland and the north part of Lancashire into a single county labelled Cumbria – still better-known as 'the Lake District' or 'Lakeland'; still associated in many people's minds as much with the poets' response to the beauties of the lakes as with the lakes themselves.

Stone cottages of Elterwater: the slate from which these cottages and walls are built probably come from the quarries close to the village lying just north of the lake.

11

Rich pastures of Little Langdale and the river Brathay.

Nowadays as Britain's largest National Park, the lakes attract millions of visitors annually. They offer opportunities for all kinds of recreation from mountaineering to scuba diving. They afford journeys of exploration and delight for fell-walkers or ramblers, and a rich cultural heritage for the contemplative; for those who live and work in the nearby cities they give a sense of freedom and unburdening, as was expressed by one visitor after a morning spent among the mountains in the last years of the nineteenth century:

If anyone finds a pack of care, labelled 'The City worries of a Manchester Man,' upon the shoulders of Skiddaw 'Laal Man,' he can let it stay there - Skiddaw's shoulders are strong enough to bear it, ay, and all the sorrows of my teeming town.

The writer, Hardwicke Rawnsley, founded the National Trust in 1895 with two fellow-conservationists, the housing reformer Octavia Hill and her adviser, a professional adminstrator,

Sir Robert Hunter. In 1905 the Trust was able to buy its first property on Derwent Water through public subscription, and it now owns nearly 134,000 acres of public land, over 40,000 acres of hill and lowland farms and 30,000 head of sheep in the Lake District alone. Skiddaw's shoulders and other mountain slopes support the sheep, and have yielded minerals and stone. For the fell farmers, life's burdens and sorrows are likely to be caused by the mountains as well as relieved by them - the former through the natural hazards of wind, snow and mist experienced by shepherds and their flocks on the ledges and crags, the latter through such pursuits as hunting or hound trailing, or fell-racing during the annual sports, and no doubt through the pleasures of an outdoor life spent among lovely and familiar scenes in the bloom of summer or the freshness of spring. For the rest of us these pleasures are to be enjoyed whenever we have time to wander, ramble the fells, or climb the lofty mountains.

1 *Orientation*

The lakes in their mountain fastness are encircled not only by natural boundaries, but by roads and railways. The two rail lines which converge on Carlisle take the only passable routes round the mountain mass. That to the east, through the beautiful Eden valley, links market towns which are the traditional outlets from the lake country or points of entry for visitors to the lakes themselves. The road and rail route along the coast, while serving the northern industrial towns, also follows the medieval packhorse routes between farms in their separate dales. Yet even these coastal routes were advocated in the fell walkers' indispensable *Baddeley* as a desirable approach for tourists:

'Wasdale, Ennerdale and Crummock can only be properly appreciated by being *first* seen from their lower ends. Wildness of scenery, to be thoroughly effective, must burst suddenly upon the eye. Disappointment is always the lot of those who walk from the grand to the tame end of a wild lake, and expect, by the simple process of turning round, to feel all its force.'

Since M J B Baddeley compiled his guide, travel and sight-seeing have changed. The first 'lakers' travelled from lake to lake by carriage and later visitors travelled by rail and then hired a conveyance to the centre of their choice, whence they rambled, wandered, boated, fished or climbed. Today's tourists arrive, and travel within the lake district, by car. This adds freedom of choice but not of movement, for in season the beauties of the place attract numbers out of all proportion to its size, or the capacities of its roads. Today's visitors are encouraged to explore, whenever possible, out of season in early summer or autumn. This is to everyone's advantage, for it is then that the rainiest months have passed.

The beautiful or historic places through which these encircling routes pass themselves reward exploration. The ancient town of Lancaster provides a southern counterpart to Carlisle as a major centre of communication, while the popular resort of Morecambe faces across its vast bay the shifting sands and shining estuaries of Cartmel and Furness on the southern fringes of the lakes. Further north, Kirkby Lonsdale affords an approach to the lower reaches of Windermere from Manchester and York. Loved by Ruskin and Turner, this busy and handsome market town is visited for its church and its medieval 'Devil's Bridge,' now closed to traffic, bestriding the river Lune which rushes over rocks beneath the town. The substantial church of St Mary the Virgin shows influence from the interior of Durham Cathedral in the carved zigzag patterns and other ornamentation on its earliest pillars and arches. Around these traces of the Norman structure standing near the site of an Anglo-Saxon church, the present building developed at intervals until the Victorian era when the restorers were at work. The lovely views of the fells, which Turner painted, and of the Lune valley, show countryside as untouched as the grey town itself.

Standing on the Lancashire border, Kirkby Lonsdale was formerly the first important southern town entered in Westmorland and is now the first in Cumbria. Further north and closer to the M6 motorway, Kendal, gateway to the southern and eastern lakes, has been Westmorland's biggest town since 1388 when the ancient town of Appleby was obliterated in a surprise raid by the Scots from which it never fully recovered. Like Kirkby Lonsdale, Kendal stands on the edge of rocky limestone uplands from which stone has been quarried to build this

The scene from Colt Crags en route to Coniston Old Man, 2635 feet, a hard walk with rewarding views over Coniston Water and the gentler south-eastern fells.

'Auld Grey Town' which has been important at least since Roman times. Town and castle occupy a strategic position beside the river Kent, the castle on its height to the east of the river built on the site of a Roman outpost, the riverside church occupying the site of an Anglo-Saxon church. The town's motto *Pannus mihi Panis*, 'Wool is my Bread,' recalls days of plenty when the medieval English wool trade was at its peak. Later the manufacture of coarse drugget in which the town specialised became well enough known for Falstaff in Shakespeare's *King Henry IV* to complain of 'three misbegotten knaves in Kendal green,' for by Shakespeare's time the export trade in raw wool had been displaced by the export of finished cloth. Kendal in its setting of limestone fells remains a town of light industry, and its flourishing market has served the rural population since 1189. Today the town gives its name to Kendal mint cake which is carried by

climbers to supply the extra energy needed in a final ascent, and is equally gratifying for onlookers. For sightseers on their way to the mountains, dales and lakes Kendal with its remaining yards and wynds, the ruined castle where Catherine Parr, surviving wife of Henry VIII, was born, and the fine Gothic church – much restored – makes a splendid prelude. Some miles to the east the former county town of Westmorland, Appleby, stands on the river Eden and on the route from north-west England to Penrith and thence Keswick, Skiddaw and Derwent Water. Appleby has always been a market town, and the annual horse fair is still an important date in the calendar for dealers and

The medieval Bridge crossing the river Lune at Kirkby Lonsdale. Said to be the work of the Devil, but an inscription added in 1673 reads 'Fear God, Honour the King'.

gypsies from all over Britain. The town occupies both banks of the river, its broad main street leading from the west bank between the church and the castle, both of which recall the life of the redoubtable Lady Anne Clifford who spent the last 17 of her 87 years restoring the family castles in the north of England, as well as repairing the churches. Her tomb is seen in St Lawrence's Church which shows additions and improvements by Lady Anne as well as over varying periods from its Norman origins, visible in the base of the tower, to Victorian times. The church holds one of England's oldest organ cases, brought from Carlisle Cathedral at the time of the Civil War. The ruin of Lady Anne's moated castle, rebuilt during the Commonwealth in defiance of Cromwell, stands high above the town. In the centre of Appleby's main street, opposite the church, is the handsome sixteenth-century Moot Hall where the Borough Council still meets, and at the upper end of the street with its Georgian buildings, grass and trees, are the almshouses which Lady Anne founded in 1651 for widows of workers on the castle. A Tuscan Column stands at either end of the street, the upper one – High Cross – carrying the inscription, 'Retain your loyalty Preserve your Rights'. Dating from the seventeenth century it is still a telling admonition for a town which belonged to Scotland before the Conquest, after which it and a large part of Cumbria suffered as disputed lands. The lush Eden valley carried raiding parties between north and south, and a number of fortified farm houses survive – while every town has its ruined castle.

The Eden valley still provides a route between the Plain of York and the north-west border lands, as it has since pre-Roman days, but the route is a peaceful one, the valley is cultivated and grazed, the river rich in salmon and trout. The villages like Kirkoswald or Great Salkeld are of the red sandstone which, broken down, provides the valley's fertile soil. Near Little Salkeld on the edge of the Pennines stands a great stone circle called Long Meg and her Daughters. Long Meg reaches about ten feet high and stands apart from the accompanying oval of 64 stones, which measures 350 yards in circumference, and is the largest stone circle after Stonehenge. It stands lonely among grasses and trees, looking across to the north Cumbrian Mountains.

The Roman road turns north at Penrith for Carlisle, and for Hadrian's Wall which extended from the Tyne on England's north-east coast to the Solway Firth where the deep broad estuary of the Esk cuts between northern Cumbria and Scotland. Carlisle was a major military base from which the Roman legions defended the vulnerable Solway Plain, keeping apart the Scottish 'Barbarians' and the Brigantes occupying the Cumbrian mountains, who were likely to join forces against the occupying Romans. The Brigantian threat was also met by establishing forts along the Cumberland coast, and by continuing defences inland across the southern ranges from the Ravenglass estuary over the precipitous Hardknott Pass to Ambleside and thence north-east along High Street, a lofty, bleak ridge stretching between Haweswater and Ullswater to the Roman fort at Brougham just south of Penrith. In this way the Lake District was contained: Carlisle guarded it and the lower lands beyond its northernmost height, High Pike. After the Roman occupation and the Norman Conquest Carlisle, far from keeping the peace between Cumbria and Scotland became England's most contested town in one of her most contested counties – now Scottish, now English. Carlisle's city walls, castle and priory – later to become its cathedral – were begun once William Rufus had regained the city from the Scots, but these were destroyed and rebuilt repeatedly over the centuries, and fragments of building and rebuilding can be seen in the ruined castle and in this, England's smallest cathedral which was finally – and sensitively – restored by the Victorians. The castle contains stones from the Norman nave of the cathedral, plundered by the Parliamentarians after they had won Carlisle in the terrible siege of 1644, by which time the cathedral had been in a ruinous state since the Dissolution of Henry VIII's reign. On the castle walls can be seen vivid and poignant carvings, perhaps carried out by a prisoner incarcerated by the Duke of Cumberland after his rout of Prince Charles Edward in the rebellion of 1745. Only in the two centuries since has this busy manufacturing and market town, county town of Cumberland and now of all Cumbria, known peace, and relics of war can be seen in the museum at Tullie House which has fragments of the original Roman city in its grounds. Inscribed stones from Hadrian's Wall are shown in the museum as well as displays of Lakeland geology and local history. At the entrance is a replica of the seventh-century Bewcastle Cross whose shaft stands in the village churchyard near the Roman Wall. Over 12 feet high, the red sandstone shaft is elaborately

Kendal's New Shambles / over 200 years old. The Old Shambles, the street of the butchers' shops, forms part of Kendal's extensive renovation scheme.

carved with biblical figures and has been described as one of the finest of its kind in Europe.

From Carlisle, or the sea-washed turf of Solway, road joins rail to follow the western coastal fringe of the Lake District where, as Camden observed, 'the Ocean driving and dashing upon the shore affourdeth plenty of excellent good fish...' Since those days the industrial ports of Maryport, Workington and Whitehaven have grown to prosper from local coal and iron and to see these industries decline. Coal and iron have been replaced by other industries including chemicals and steel, engineering, fishing and tourism. Whitehaven and Maryport are fundamentally Georgian towns which were active in the Middle Ages while Workington developed during the Industrial Revolution: lacking the purely picturesque attractions of other coastal resorts, they avoid also the sense of impermanence felt in places whose sole activity depends on the seasonal tourist trade. The coast too, marked by industry and by traffic routes, still has good sands,

golf-courses, the beautiful St Bees Head and the Drigg nature reserve, and 'plenty of excellent good fish,' while the railway-age resort of Seascale caters for, and sends workers to, the atomic reactors at Calder Hall and Windscale. Aesthetically at least, these futuristic intrusions upon the western fells have been accepted by many as striking additions to the landscape rather than unsightly ones. Meanwhile, minor roads answering the call of the mountains ranged on the skyline lead, as Baddeley prescribed, to Crummock Water and to Buttermere, Ennerdale and Wast Water and thence to the lakes' wild heart. From the village of Ravenglass, whose main street and houses dip their feet in the sea, a modern road follows the Roman route across Hardknott and Wrynose Passes between stern Sca Fell and the gentler Duddon valley, revered by Wordsworth, while the Eskdale and Ravenglass Miniature Railway 'La'al Ratty' so-called, it is said, because it rattles, carries visitors (where it once carried iron ore) on a magnificent scenic ride from Ravenglass to Dalegarth near Boot, seven

miles up-dale. Ravenglass on its three-pronged estuary at the convergence of the rivers Irt, Mite and Esk, looks across at the sand dunes of Drigg Point which is formed by the estuary of the Irt, and where Britain's largest colony of black-headed gulls breeds. Between the sea cliffs and the valleys of the Mite and Esk, shrouded in woodland, are the 12-foot pinkish walls of the bath-house which is all that remains of the Roman fort Glannaventa. Known as Walls Castle, the ruin is among the tallest Roman structures standing in Britain. It might have been a source of interest to the builders of the peel tower, owned by the Pennington family, which in the Middle Ages afforded protection to the family as well as local people and their livestock against border raiders and which the Penningtons later commissioned the celebrated Salvin to incorporate into the gracious and comfortable dwelling now known as Muncaster Castle. Salvin's nineteenth-century *tour de force*, which holds the family's collection of fine furniture and works of art, stands in terraced gardens which are

vivid with rhododendron in summer, and famous for their vistas along the Esk valley with its backing of dark mountain peaks.

Between the estuary sands at Ravenglass and the Duddon estuary which bites northward further down the coast a southern spur from the lakeland dome protrudes seaward and

Appleby Horse Fair, held on the second Tuesday and Wednesday in June, has been a major attraction for gypsies from all parts of Britain and Ireland since 1685.

19

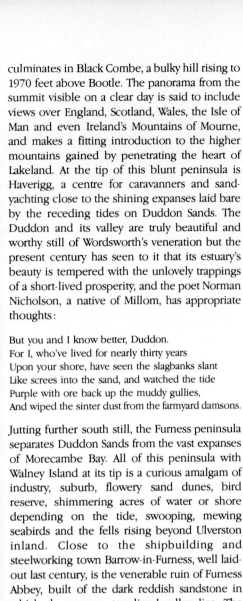

culminates in Black Combe, a bulky hill rising to 1970 feet above Bootle. The panorama from the summit visible on a clear day is said to include views over England, Scotland, Wales, the Isle of Man and even Ireland's Mountains of Mourne, and makes a fitting introduction to the higher mountains gained by penetrating the heart of Lakeland. At the tip of this blunt peninsula is Haverigg, a centre for caravanners and sand-yachting close to the shining expanses laid bare by the receding tides on Duddon Sands. The Duddon and its valley are truly beautiful and worthy still of Wordsworth's veneration but the present century has seen to it that its estuary's beauty is tempered with the unlovely trappings of a short-lived prosperity, and the poet Norman Nicholson, a native of Millom, has appropriate thoughts:

But you and I know better, Duddon.
For I, who've lived for nearly thirty years
Upon your shore, have seen the slagbanks slant
Like screes into the sand, and watched the tide
Purple with ore back up the muddy gullies,
And wiped the sinter dust from the farmyard damsons.

Jutting further south still, the Furness peninsula separates Duddon Sands from the vast expanses of Morecambe Bay. All of this peninsula with Walney Island at its tip is a curious amalgam of industry, suburb, flowery sand dunes, bird reserve, shimmering acres of water or shore depending on the tide, swooping, mewing seabirds and the fells rising beyond Ulverston inland. Close to the shipbuilding and steelworking town Barrow-in-Furness, well laid-out last century, is the venerable ruin of Furness Abbey, built of the dark reddish sandstone in which the narrow, tree-lined valley lies. The substantial remains of the abbey are cared for and their grounds tended by the Department of the Environment but as Norman Nicholson wrote, 'It does not need ornament, however; it does not need legends, nor ivy and hanging plants. It achieves dignity, solid and simple as Gregorian plainsong. It was built sternly for its purpose – as functional in design as a blast-furnace.'

On the north-eastern edge of the Furness peninsula the rivers Crake and Leven pour from Coniston and Windermere to meet over Cartmel Sands. Into Morecambe Bay protrudes the mass of land, due south of Windermere, on which the Victorian resort of Grange-over-Sands, and the remains of Cartmel Priory stand. This is more fertile country than the bleak mountains and it

Peaceful pastoral scenery of the Eden Valley, whose river waters abound in salmon and trout.

has long been a source of wealth. After the Dissolution the twelfth-century priory fell into decay but its church was beautifully restored in the seventeenth century by George Preston of Holker Hall. Its elaborate and amusing misericords are one of many delights and its village, Cartmel, another: the thirteenth-century priory gatehouse, strongly fortified, belongs to the National Trust and serves as an information centre. Holker Hall nearby is a stately home of the seventeenth century still occupied by the Cavendish family, who inherited it in 1756. Its deer park and gardens, overlooking Morecambe Bay, are as beautiful as its interior which shows outstanding local craftsmanship and contains a rich collection of furniture and paintings set in a series of exquisitely decorated rooms. Further east in the valley of the river Kent, between Kendal and the Kent estuary, stands the Elizabethan Levens Hall in its famous topiary gardens, its elaborate plasterwork ceilings and decorated leather panelling reflecting the social and historic changes that had come about since its earliest walls were built in 1300 as a peel tower. A mile or so north, Sizergh Castle's fourteenth-century peel tower remains the core to which its grand hall is a substantial addition. The hall's interior shows local Elizabethan craftsmanship at its peak; fine furniture and paintings fill the rooms, and a small museum is

run by the National Trust, which owns the property, on the top floor of the peel tower. A little to the east of the well-tended gardens the A6 runs northward through damson orchards toward Kendal, gateway to Windermere, and gateway to the lakes.

Opposite Carlisle Cathedral, restored in the mid-nineteenth century but still showing part of the original Norman nave with stone from the Roman Wall. The tower was added in 1401.

Below Border fortress: Carlisle Castle, partially ruined after capture by the Scots in 1216 and since rebuilt, now holds the Border Regiment Museum.

Overleaf Remote Crummock Water lies under scooped-out hillsides divided by Scale Beck.

High summer at Leven's Hall brings a blaze of flowers to this Elizabethan mansion's famous topiary gardens.

Opposite Summer's evening at Buttermere where Chapel Crags tower like a vertical wall over Burtness woods.

Eroded red sandstone walls of Furness Abbey, endowed by King Stephen in 1127 for the Savignac Order. Later, as a Cistercian house, Furness became the foremost abbey in north-west England.

2 Wandering

The names 'Windermere' or poetic 'Winandermere' from original variations on the Norse 'Vinand's Lake' are well-suited to this gently serpentine water, England's largest lake, in its pastoral setting amid the lower fells with glimpses of greater heights beyond. Over ten miles long and rarely more than a mile wide Windermere thrusts its snout into the sterner volcanic ranges around Ambleside – Wansfell, Rydal and Loughrigg – from which its waters meander southward through the milder Silurian hills to Cartmel. Like Windermere, Coniston lying to westward is edged with pastures and woods, although Dunnerdale Fells and Coniston's quarry-scarred Old Man accompany its western shore. Beyond Windermere's head the small lakes of Rydal and Grasmere and a confluence of many rivers winding in their broad and fertile dales allow untaxing excursions amid woods and farmland overlooked by fell, how, pike and crag – lofty inspirations for the wanderer in the valleys. This makes a pleasant introduction to the lakes, for without too much effort fine views can be obtained by ascending vantage-points well-documented since the appearance of the first popular *Guides*, among them Wordsworth's and Harriet Martineau's. Here too can be followed the paths of these famous 'off-comers,' the lake poets and chroniclers and their friends; their houses may be visited, and their graves; the natural inspiration for their poems and essays contemplated at source. Predictably the present century has broken the sense of remoteness and solitude by introducing motor boats and major roads notably along the larger lakes, through which the scenic and literary pilgrimage threatens, in season, to defeat its own ends. Windermere with its island, ferry, steamboat excursions, sailing clubs and scuba diving, invaluable National Park Visitor Centre and incomparable railway approach is the most welcoming of lakes, and has been since the days of the writers and poets, who recorded earlier diversions. William Gilpin described char fishing, 'A parcel of char, just caught, and thrown together into the luggage-boot of a boat, makes a pleasant harmony of colouring': H D Rawnsley reminisced about skating on Windermere,

Here, a pony with its jangling sleigh bells dashed along; there, fond fathers pushed their little ones in perambulators. A hurdy gurdy man made music here, and yonder, on St Mary's Holme, a brass band blew its best, and risked frozen lips and frost-bitten fingers in the process. Tea, one was reminded, was obtainable here; oranges were possible there.

By contrast, one hot summer, Scott visited the self-styled Admiral of the Lakes, the poet, wrestler, athlete and ascerbic journalist John Wilson, or 'Christopher North' who fêted Scott on Windermere. A member of the great man's party later recorded the scene where

The three Bards of the Lakes led the cheers that hailed Scott and Canning; and the music and sunshine, flags, streamers, and gay dresses, the merry hum of voices, and the rapid splashings of innumerable oars, made up a dazzling mixture of sensations, as the flotilla wound its way among richly-foliaged islands, and along bays and promontories peopled with enthusiastic spectators.

The 'richly-foliaged islands,' the bays and the promontories, are indeed best appreciated from the water. Practical Harriet Martineau details the boat trip for the visitor: 'In accordance with the rule of the lake approach, we should recommend his going down first. He embarks at the pier at

Dominating Coniston
Water's western shore,
the stony fells climbing
from the lakeside
provide walking and
clambering where once
they yielded copper and
stone.

Bowness. ...Then the course is southwards, with the lake narrowing, and the hills sinking till the scenery becomes merely pretty.' These two extremes in beauty can be experienced in the same manner today from Bowness, a pleasant and busy lakeside resort situated close to the town of Windermere half-way along the lake's bank. For motorists, a car ferry further south links the hilly minor road from Kendal with a steep drive which skirts Claife Heights, passes Beatrix Potter's farm at Near Sawrey and follows fertile farmland along Esthwaite's reedy waters to Hawkshead (a favoured walk of the Words-worths) and thence over Hawkshead Hill, around the head of Coniston Water to its village. The Bowness ferry also carries walkers who wish to follow Windermere's peaceful western shore through 'merely pretty' woodland, or to walk north beneath Claife Heights toward the National Trust's Wray Castle, a nineteenth-century addition, 'a most defensible-looking place for so peaceful a region' comments wry Miss Martineau. From here can be seen sweeping views across the lake's head and Ambleside. Ramblers standing on Jenkyn's Crag below Wansfell, themselves part of this view, will look across at the neo-Tudor bulk of Wray Castle in its rhododendrons, at the woods and fells, and Windermere's blue ribbon winding south as far as Belle Isle and Bowness. To the north-west is the distant craggy sculpture of the Langdale Pikes.

Just below Ambleside to the west of Waterhead where the Brathay enters the lake stood the Roman fort of Galava, and it is supposed that building stone was brought up-lake by boat just as goods have been carried for centuries between lakeside communities, and iron ore from mines for smelting in Windermere's thick woodlands. Ambleside itself is a pleasant touring centre, an old town couched in wooded fells set near the meeting point of numerous rivers and dales, with the waters of nearby lakes lying unseen to north, south and west. Chief of Ambleside's sights are the tiny seventeenth-century Bridge House which the National Trust has opened as an information centre, and a water-wheel surviving from one of the town's many former mills. Literary associations are centred on the home of the sociologist and writer Harriet Martineau, which she called the Knoll, where besides giving lecture courses for local children and adults and founding a workers' building society, she kept open house for her neighbours and for such literary visitors as Charlotte Brontë, George Eliot

Late winter snow still clings to the Rydal Fells beyond the Vale of Grasmere.

33

and Mrs Gaskell. Favoured rambles around Ambleside include Jenkyn's Crag or the 70-foot Stock Ghyll Force, reached by ascending some way east of town. Miss Martineau in her *Guide* suggests 'If his time in Ambleside is precious, the stranger may use the sunset or twilight hour for seeing Stock Ghyll Force, while his supper is preparing' but an earlier visitor, John Keats, obviously had no directions for reaching the site since he wrote, 'We, I may say, fortunately, missed the direct path, and after wandering a little, found it out by the noise…the waterfall itself, which I came suddenly upon, gave me a pleasant twinge.' He describes the sight: 'the different falls have as different characters; the first darting down the slate rock like an arrow; the second spreading out like a fan – the third dashed into a mist – and one on the other side of the rock a sort of mixture of all these.'

The Knoll stands near the noisy major highway which has hugged Windermere's east bank and leads through Ambleside to follow the banks of Rydal Water and Grasmere before climbing bleak Dunmail Raise to Thirlmere and the northern lakes. The River Rothay, following the road and linking the lakes in their fells, pours out of Rydal's eastward head to flow across Ambleside's broad vale before joining the Brathay and entering Windermere. Road and river follow ancient routes immortalised by the poets in whose footsteps countless literary pilgrims tread. Rydal village, with Wordsworth's last home about two hundred yards further up, lies in woods at the eastern end of this small, reedy, beautiful lake; here the great man lived in his old age, his inspiration spent, his fame assured: hundreds of admirers visited him at Rydal Mount. Behind the village church, whose site Wordsworth helped to choose, is the field he gave to his daughter Dora; it is a National Trust property and in spring a golden mass of daffodils. Toward Nab Cottage and Grasmere an isolated crag, 'Wordsworth's Seat,' contemplates the waters below. Perhaps it was this once peaceful spot that Wordsworth had in mind when, in his *Guide to the Lakes*, he wrote of 'that placid and quiet feeling which belongs peculiarly to the lake – as a body of still water under the influence of no current; reflecting therefore the clouds, the light, and all the imagery of the sky and the surrounding hills.' Further on from here is the cottage where Coleridge's son Hartley, whom Wordsworth looked on almost as his own, came to live an unsatisfactory existence as a failed poet for 12 years before his death in 1849. Earlier the poet Thomas De Quincey courted a farmer's daughter

here, and earned the disapproval of the Wordsworths by marrying her: she helped him control his opium habit, and cared for him until her death 20 years later. So the poets lived, while the dalesmen continued their traditional skills, shepherding, sheep-washing, sheep-clipping and enjoyed their traditional pastimes of fox hunting, village sports meetings and wrestling, while supplementing their income by acting as guides to ramblers and fell-walkers. Two different views of Rydal come down to us from those days, one immortalised in these lines from F W Faber's poem about Rydal Vale:

The hills with vernal green were gently flushed,
And every sound about the place was hushed,
Except the blue lake softly murmuring.

The other is related by Edwin Waugh in his essay, also called *Rydal Vale*, in which he gives an account of a walk from Grasmere in the company of an old fell-farmer:

About a mile on our way we came out upon the open road, at a point from whence the whole extent of the lively lake, called 'Rydal Water,' with its green islets, and its picturesque shores, lay full in view of us, sleeping calmly in its verdant nest, at the foot of the wild mountains. Here we paused a little, to gaze upon the scene – which is very beautiful. The old farmer felt its charm, too, for, after gazing upon it silently for a little while, he said very quietly, as we turned away, that it was 'sartinly a verra bonnie laal lake.'

Grasmere, 'the loveliest spot that man hath ever found,' lies at the head of a broad and fertile dale which has Rydal Fell on its eastern flank, Blea Rigg and Silver How along its south-west edge, and Helm Crag protruding from the north-west to divide the vale at its northern end. Easedale Gill flows along the dale's western prong to meet the Rothay just above Grasmere village where Wordsworth's Dove Cottage was visited by Edwin Waugh on his walk to Rydal: 'a substantial, roomy, old-fashioned cottage, in good condition, newly whitewashed, and with clean windows, with flower pots peeping in through the lowmost panes'. Here William and his sister Dorothy lived, walked the dales and lower fells, entertained Coleridge, Southey, De Quincey, and worked – he on his poems and she, after the housekeeping, on her *Journals*: '…I observed the glittering silver line on the ridge of the backs of the sheep, owing to their situation respecting the sun, which made them look beautiful, but with something of strangeness, like animals of another kind, as if belonging to a more splendid world.' The Wordsworths lived here for

Old Bridge House in Ambleside. Built in the eighteenth century as a summer house, it now serves as an Information Centre for the National Trust.

Overleaf The start of an arduous climb over the Derwent Fells from sheltered pastures around the western shores of the lake. 35

a time after William's marriage to Mary Hutchinson of Penrith, and later when they and Dorothy and the growing family had moved to a roomier dwelling nearby De Quincey moved to Dove Cottage. Today the house is preserved as a Wordsworthian museum, furnished as it had been when he lived here producing his greatest work and as yet unrecognised. In the village church, outwardly rather plain, where the Wordsworths worshipped, village children still celebrate the ancient rushbearing ceremony that their neighbours also observe in Ambleside; and the annual Grasmere sports today draw crowds of thousands. The simple graves of Wordsworth and his wife, and of Wordsworth's daughter whose death as a young married woman brought grief to Rydal Mount, are also a source of pilgrimage.

Just over 20 years after Wordsworth's death in 1850 the writer, artist and social reformer John Ruskin bought a house on Coniston's eastern shore, and here at Brantwood he lived until his death in 1900, aged 81. He completed his autobiography here, and his collection of minerals. He revived cottage industries at Elterwater and Keswick, mingled with the villagers, looked out at the quarried and weathered form of the Coniston Old Man: 'Today' – writing in February 1883 – 'really rather bright blue, and bright semi-cumuli, with the frantic Old Man blowing sheaves of lancets and chisels across the lake...'. Of the winter some five years earlier he had recorded that it was 'one of the most healthy and lovely I ever saw ice in; Coniston lake shone under the calm clear frost in one marble field, as strong as the floor of Milan Cathedral...' In the Ruskin Museum at the former mining and present stone-quarrying village of Coniston, just across the water, Ruskin's personal memorabilia can be seen among his pictures and writings, and his collection of minerals. In the churchyard an elaborately carved cross commemorates the area's most celebrated resident. On the village green a slate seat from the Coniston quarries commemorates a celebrated visitor, Donald Campbell, who spent many years continuing his father's successful attempts to raise the world water speed record over this long narrow tree-fringed slit of water, and who died in so doing in January 1967, at the age of 36. His grave is the rocky depth of the lake. Like Windermere, Coniston Water is an ancient public thoroughfare but it is less accessible and therefore less-frequented, much of its beauty lying in the contrast between its low, rounded, pastoral fells that rise directly over the eastern shore and the higher, rugged range that follows the meadows along its western bank. One of the lake's more accessible beauty spots, much-visited, is Tarn Hows high up on the western fells from which can be seen an exquisite tree-fringed tarn lying among the hills at the head of the lake – an exercise in perfection, the small shallow mere reflecting the moods and varying aspects of woods and mountains and skies. The tarn, three pools joined early this century and planted with larches and evergreen, shows a collaboration between nature and man. Other lonelier, quite as lovely, tarns lie in clefts amid the mountains and fells nearby, for those who wish to seek them out. With a little exertion – taking the popular quarry route – wanderers can ascend the Coniston Old Man, 2635 feet high, and feel that they have climbed a mountain.

From here to south and west can be seen the distant coast beyond field and fell with Duddon Sands glimmering, and the *couchant* Black Combe; a confusion of wilder higher mountains to north and west: High Street marching away north-east, and the full stretch of Coniston Water below. Immediately west the summit of Dow Crag calls all climbers. Held in the arms of Dow Crag and the Old Man, although not visible from here, is Goat's – or Gait's – Water 'The wildest of all the tarns,' according to E Lynn Linton writing her *Lake Country* in 1864, 'hidden away under the bleak rocks of Dow Crags, like the very wreckage of creation and the spoils of a world foregone'. Beyond this range, on its westward side, the lovely Duddon runs down. This was Wordsworth's favourite river and he dedicated a series of 34 sonnets to the Duddon Valley, the last of which seems appropriate to any setting, be it along the ferny river bank or the sea-swept sands, contemplating the bleak mountain scarp, or back in the cities and towns from which we pour to walk or float or climb among Cumbria's lakes.

I thought of thee, my partner and my guide,
As being passed away – Vain sympathies!
For, backward, Duddon, as I cast my eyes,
I see what was, and is, and will abide;
Still glides the Stream, and shall for ever glide;
The Form remains, the Function never dies;
While we, the brave, the mighty, and the wise,
We Men, who in our morn of youth defied
The elements, must vanish; be it so!
Enough, if something from our hands have power
To live, and act, and serve the future hour;
And if, as toward the silent tomb we go,
Through love, through hope, and faith's transcendent dower,
We feel that we are greater than we know.

3 Climbing Country

Mountaineering was born a British sport, and the Lake District of the late nineteenth century was its nursery. Since those infant days the sport has broken down into varying activities, the most hazardous being mountaineering or rock climbing, or its winter equivalent ice climbing, each of which has its own unwritten rules and lore. The mountaineer's objective is to achieve a summit by a chosen route, while rock climbers will seek ever-harsher challenges on cliff or rock faces, often in areas where there are no mountains. Over the years names of men and rock faces have gone down in the Lakeland annals, new codes have emerged with fresh challenges and new techniques, or cast-off codes have been lamented but later revived. Recently F J Carruthers wrote of a fresh attempt in 1892 on Sca Fell's Moss Ghyll. 'It was the first recorded use of an artificial aid in rock climbing. Climbers were expected to get up without such aids, by using the powers God had given them, of muscle and balance.' The informal code of conduct which emerged in the early days was not restricted to the rock face itself. For many years one frowned on 'the fellow who wore nailed boots and slung rope in Keswick's Main Street' – no, the climber 'would go to the spot selected as the start point of a climbing expedition in conservative dress, and only emerge complete with nailed boots and climbing rope on the fellside.' Nowadays few people would set out for the mountains clad in a suit, while artificial aids which were widely used in the '50s and early '60s are resorted to only on routes that are the most extreme of those graded 'extremely severe.' The climbers again rely on their God-given powers, employing complex 'protection systems' of rope which prevent falls but give no other assistance. Even in its infancy, the sport was seeing new generations of *aficionados* whose attitudes differed from those of the old, as Lord Chorley's essay 'Some Notes on Pillar History' showed in an account of the Revd James Jackson's first ascent in 1875 of the notorious Pillar Rock at the age of 79 and a successful ascent the following year, at 80. '...of his tragic death beneath the shadow of the Rock,' concludes the writer, 'I have not space to tell. His passing coincided with a new era, the era of the expert rock climber, who sought new routes for the sake of climbing, and not merely in order to reach the summit.'

The summits of all the lakes' lofty mountains can be reached by the hale and hearty hiker, but there are routes which only experienced climbers can attempt. Besides mountaineering, rock climbing and ice climbing there are various fell-walking activities, which include the gruelling Fell-Walking Marathon as well as 'doing a Wainwright' – ascending, or 'bagging,' the 214 fell tops included in A Wainwright's 7 classic *Pictorial Guides to the Lakeland Fells* – or attaining membership of the Bob Graham Club (which celebrated its half-century in 1982) by 'bagging' a given number of peaks in 24 hours. Mountaineering and rock climbing are still sports with no written rules, apart from the grading scales which are almost universally recognised. The English grading ranges from 'Easy' or 'Moderate' for scramblers, to 'Extremely Severe' which only a handful of the most skilled climbers have managed, and can be found on rock faces of the Sca Fell, Great Gable and Langdale groups, where the rock climber's most rewarding days are spent. E F Bosman, writing in *British Hills and Mountains*, distinguished the climber's territory thus:

...if on a fine day you fall off, or on a day of gale or rain are blown off, the Striding Edge, you will not roll down

Fell Foot descending to Little Langdale from Wrynose Pass. The glacially scooped valleys of Great and Little Langdale penetrate westward from the quiet beauty of the south-eastern lakes into the bleak drama of Cumbria's highest peaks.

to Red Tarn on one side or to Grisedale on the other… If, however, you overstep a precipice on Sca Fell, or any of his lords-in-waiting – Great Gable or Bowfell or Pavey Ark or the Langdales – then nothing will save you except your two hands and feet; if you fall you will be killed.

This hazardous pastime is fascinating to watch, and in season the climbers have come to form part of the landscape even more than the fell-walkers, hikers and excursionists who transform the lakes and mountains by filling the landscape with figures. The climbers, moving with slow deliberation, seem to have something in common with the fell-farmer and dalesman. In a transient rôle they too are pitted against the immovable mountains and the ever-changing elements.

The climbers' territory lies in the wild south-western regions where few roads pass, and footpaths following pack-horse routes lead high into the crowding mountains' heart. Once you are surrounded on all sides by England's highest ranges – Sca Fell, Great Gable, Pillar and the Langdale Pikes, with their lesser but no less awe-inspiring companions Bow Fell, Great End, or Crinkle Crags – a network of footpaths between lead to the passes that form crossroads for climbers and fell-walkers. Sty Head Pass, Black Sail and Esk Hause are well-trodden and well-used, and it has been said that you would meet every cragsman of note if you waited long enough at Sty Head Pass. From the outlying regions around the coast, long arms of valleys reach their lakes in the centre. Wast Water and Eskdale lead from the south-west to the Sca Fell and Great Gable groups while lonely Ennerdale arrives at Kirk Fell and Great Gable from the west. Roads following Wast Water and Ennerdale peter out as they approach the central *massif*; Eskdale's road skirts Wast Water and the foot of the Sca Fell range and leads south-east over the Romans' Hard Knott Pass, bleak high country, to the head of the river Duddon and Cockley Beck. The road climbs again to reach Wrynose Pass, and here the Three Shire Stone marks the place where you can step between Lancashire, Cumberland and Westmorland. The road enters Little Langdale with its velvety-green hillsides, and leads to Elter

Water and the south-eastern lakes. From Keswick by way of Derwent Water and Borrowdale you can drive southward along one of the earlier tourists' carriage routes which daringly penetrates the stony heart of the mountains under the glare of Glaramara but quickly turns back on itself over Honister Pass to find Buttermere below, and follows the lake along its northern edge. Across the moody waters are skyline views of High Stile and its consorts High Crag and Red Pike, with white slithers of waterfalls dropping from the clifftops. The road crosses the wedge of pastureland that separates Buttermere from Crummock Water, and makes its way along the lower lake to Lorton Vale, and Cockermouth. Another popular and beautiful route starts at the mouth of Great Langdale and leads through rich grazing land to ever-barer and higher and wilder country, ending at the mountain rescue post under the Langdale Pikes. An alternative approach is to take a minor – very minor – road climbing northward out of Little Langdale in a series of swoops which reveal the startling panorama of Great Langdale's Pike o' Stickle, the higher but less striking 'pike,' Harrison Stickle, the climbers' Gimmer Crag between, and steep Pavey Ark. Walkers can explore Dungeon Ghyll – 60 feet of mare's tail frothing or roaring, depending on the weather, in a chasm no more than three feet wide held between 100-foot cliffs, isolating Harrison Stickle. The pass and the Pikes make this one of the memorable gateways to the inner mountains.

Baddeley's advice about approaching Wasdale was followed, prematurely, by Samuel Taylor Coleridge, the most adventurous of the Lake poets. Starting near the foot of Wast Water he took the road that follows through woodland and fields until the hard beauty of Wast Water and the Screes makes its appearance on the approach to Wast Water's western edge. Coleridge, who was on a lone August expedition during which he made the first recorded ascent of Sca Fell, entered in his notebook this description of the lake with its Screes:

…and when first I came, the lake was like a mirror, & conceive what the reflections must have been, of this huge facing of rock, more than half a mile of direct (perpendicular) height, with deep perpendicular Ravins, from the Top two thirds down other Ravins slanted athwart down them the whole wrinkled & torrent-torn and barely-patched with Moss – and all this reflected, turned in Pillars, & a whole new world of images, in the water…

From this approach there unfolds a classic Lakeland view of Wasdale Head's lonely pastures and stone walls hemmed in on the left by Yewbarrow's sharp edge and on the right by Lingmell and by Scafell Pike, with Great Gable framed between. The reverse view from Great Gable's Sphinx Rock is no less awesome, for the green patchwork of Wasdale Head forms a contrast with the sombre waters of the lake walled in by the Screes and Yewbarrow's bulk, with Middle Fell and Buckbarrow diminishing beyond. From Great Gable's summit most of Lakeland's mountain system comes into view, with the sea everchanging in the south-west. Wasdale village in its high, isolated valley is reputed to have the smallest church in England and towering Scafell Pike is England's highest mountain while Wast Water, scooped to below sea-level by glaciers, is England's deepest lake. The churchyard holds the graves of climbers lost on the slopes, and the mountain tops carry war memorials to the dead of both World Wars. A well-remembered name in the locality is Will Ritson, master of the hunt and landlord of the Wast Water Hotel, who died in 1890. '…an intercourse with every class of society,' explained Baddeley, 'had not the slightest perceptible influence in changing his manners or his dialect.' It was for these manners that he was celebrated as 'one of the last representatives of a type of Englishman which has, alas, been "civilised" out of the country – the "Cumberland statesman".' This gifted story-teller and conversationalist was described by the pioneer rock climber W P Haskett Smith as 'a real artist in words, in grouping, in light and shade, in colour, and in dramatic climax' – a description that could be applied equally to Ritson's mountain home.

Haskett Smith was the first to scale Great Gable's Napes Needle, a huge detached jag of rock topped by a slightly overhanging block, in 1886:

My first care was to get two or three stones and test the flatness of the summit by seeing whether anything thrown-up could be induced to lodge. If it did, that would be an indication of a moderately flat top, and would hold out hopes of the edge being found not too much rounded to afford a good grip for the fingers. Out of three missiles one consented to stay, and thereby encouraged me to start, feeling as small as a mouse climbing a milestone.

The milestone and its mountain, and the lofty Sca Fells, offer stern testing ground for climbers,

Lakeland's stony heart where Sca Fell and Scafell Pike reign over the mountain wilderness of the region's remote south-west. Scafell Pike, 3210 feet, is England's geatest height.

notably on Sca Fell's savage north face, while scramblers take a tough route up Lords Rake and walkers approach from the milder western slopes. Broad Strand separates the two mountains of Sca Fell and its brother whose Scafell Pike, 3210 feet, is England's highest point. Broad Strand is only for climbers, although Coleridge approached it with little thought or fear: 'I began to suspect that I ought not to go on; but then unfortunately, though I could with ease drop down a smooth rock of 7 feet high, I could not *climb* it, so go on I must; and go on I went'. In the days before the formation of the National Park and mountain rescue teams, the few people who approached the mountains with Coleridge's joy and impulsiveness sometimes got into difficulties which cost their lives or the lives of villagers who came to their aid. The bleak and stony summit of Scafell Pike, which is one of three 'pikes,' or peaks, on the same mountain, has varying ascents of which the approach from Borrowdale via Esk Hause, according to Wainwright's fourth *Guide*, 'is the finest. The transition from the quiet beauty of the valley pastures and woods to the rugged wildness of the

mountain top is complete…' On a lower ridge a Neolithic flint works has been found; the Romans were not the first to establish routes over this difficult country, and the art of mountain climbing probably began from the time men stood upright, and first recognised the irresistible challenge of the heights.

Another famous detached crag whose challenging form stands out as a landmark on the slopes of its wild valley, Ennerdale, is Pillar Rock which stands below the summit of Pillar Fell, and was possibly the first 'extremely severe' climb of recent times to be mastered. Climbing as an organised sport was yet to be thought of in 1826 when newspapers carried a paragraph about the feat, performed by John Atkinson of Ennerdale.

…his dog, the faithful attendant of the shepherd, lay by his staff at the bottom, and as if conscious of the danger his master was incurring by the attempt, uttered the most piteous cries during his absence…the only precaution he took for his descent was placing pieces of moss on the track by which he ascended.

Fell-walkers as well as climbers are urged to take suitable precautions these days, for all can fall foul of the weather, which in the mountains can

be predicted only by those who work among them – and generally it is only those for whom the land provides a livelihood who would claim to know it well enough to walk it without compass or map. There are innumerable well-documented walks among these mountains, each with its individual charm, whether it be a sudden view of savage majesty or, as in an ascent of Red Pike, the scene of lake waters – Buttermere and distant Crummock – that can vary from glowing blue to steely grey or wind-tossed brown, depending on the weather, the time of day or even the passing of clouds. Buttermere's becks are well-known, and the pack-horse track coming up from the coast over Sty Head Pass, linking Wast Water, Sca Fell and Great Gable with Borrowdale, is a favourite route. Glaramara's ridge system, a Y-shape with Glaramara at its centre and the prongs thrusting towards Borrowdale, provides caves, a ghyll, climbing crags and a tarn, and the most charming views over Borrowdale and Derwent Water can be gained from the ascent via Esk Hause. 'This excursion,' advised Baddeley, 'will occupy about 6 hours. A pleasant addition is to climb Great End

from the top of Esk Hause, the little extra exertion being more than compensated for by the glorious view.' At the head of Derwent Water, and the foot of Borrowdale, there is a good vantage-point from which to watch climbers tackling Shepherd's Crag; but Borrowdale and Derwent Water, Helvellyn and Skiddaw, set in the north-eastern band of the smoother Skiddaw slates, attract mainly fell-walkers and ramblers.

Striding Edge curves above Red Tarn on Helvellyn, arguably the lakes' most romantic mountain and the loftiest of the region's north-east ranges.

Overleaf Scooped by glaciers: the northern branch of Great Langdale wends toward Mickleden between the mass of Bowfell, on the left, and the climbers' delights of Pike o' Stickle, Harrison Stickle and Pavey Ark.

43

4 Rambling

The climber's reward is not the view from the top, but joy at getting there. For memorable views it is not necessary to leave the rich variety of the valleys and lakes. One of Lakeland's most beautiful valleys is Borrowdale, Derwent Water one of its loveliest lakes, and Keswick, at the foot of the lake, one of its most interesting and strikingly situated towns. Borrowdale reaches green prongs deep into the heart of the high mountains, starting at the broad foot of Derwent Water where the river Derwent enters the lake. To the east, Watendlath Beck comes tumbling from the pretty hamlet with its fine pack-horse bridge and its tarn sitting beneath Grange Fell which lies between the village and the valley, half-way toward the mountains. The village of Watendlath belongs to the National Trust, and was one of many in Borrowdale that Hugh Walpole used as a setting for his books. The bridge is a well-preserved example of those that were built, probably by farmers, when Elizabeth I's mining ventures were bringing prosperity to the region. The lower part of Watendlath Beck, near Shepherd's Crag and the lake, falls as the spectacular Lodore Cascade which, in a long poem written for his children, Southey described as

> Flying and flinging,
> Writhing and wringing,
> Eddying and whisking,
> Spouting and frisking,

and much more in the same unquenchable vein. Further up the valley a diversion can be taken in the form of a footpath which climbs away from picturesque Grange Village and through Troutdale Cottages to ascend Grange Fell. The northward prospect of valley and lake is only surpassed by the southward view of Stonethwaite

Beck meeting the waters of the Derwent before the river enters the Jaws of Borrowdale, a narrowing valley formed by Grange Fell and the westward Low Scawdel; beyond, the sky is filled with mountains – Glaramara, Great Gable, Sca Fell and their attendant peaks. King's How on Grange Fell was purchased as a memorial to King Edward VII, and carries an inscribed slab of Borrowdale slate. Just below King's How, in the valley, is the Bowder stone which as something of a curiosity is one of Borrowdale's attractions for visitors. A vast boulder, it balances in a top-heavy manner with its greater area uppermost, and is thought to have been swept into the valley by the glacier which scoured it out. Further up on the other side, Castle Crag has traces of a Roman fort and pretty views of the riverside through trees. As the valley reaches further towards the mountains it broadens to accommodate the river and the beck; the village of Rosthwaite sits between, beside a road which links the fells and the rivers. Under the height of Glaramara and its two long ridges the valley itself divides, each green strand probing further south into the precincts of the high hills. The road that has followed from Keswick turns westward at the quarrying village of Seatoller for Honister Pass and Buttermere. At the head of the westward valley by the river Derwent and overlooked on all sides by mountains is Seathwaite, which holds the

Friar's Crag, one of Lakeland's best-loved viewpoints. Ruskin's excursion to this part of Derwent Water as a child was to inspire his lifelong love of the lakes.

unenviable reputation for being the wettest settlement in England. It has been observed, however, that the rain does not fall more frequently, but simply falls harder. It is not difficult to imagine Borrowdale as an extension of its lake, as has been known after flooding rain when the river has overflowed and claimed the entire valley, for as an old saying goes 'when it siles down reet gaily, every road becomes a sike, and every sike a beck, and every beck a river.'

Like the valley, the lake has favoured places to which visitors return time and again. Derwent Water is rectangular rather than serpentine, although if it had not been separated from its northern neighbour Bassenthwaite by a large tract of marshy pastureland formed by glacial deposits the pair would make the largest, longest and broadest lake of all. The Derwent Fells and Castlerigg Fell enclose the southern lake on its eastern and western shores while to the north the waters are surrounded by pastureland, itself walled in by the fells that are never far off. Looming over the head of Derwent Water and Keswick is Skiddaw and its massive mountain block that presides over the lake system from the northern edge. Skiddaw, 3053 feet, looks south-west across the lake and the valley at the high craggy peaks of the volcanic range while its partner Saddleback, sitting east of Skiddaw, stares south-eastward over Thirlmere and Ullswater, and at Helvellyn between.

All these lakes were visited by the Lakeland *literati* of the nineteenth century. For Ruskin the view from Friars Crag on Derwent Water, a renowned beauty spot, was the 'fifth-finest in Europe', and by many other visitors it is favoured above all other in the Lake District as a symphony of trees, stone, reflection and distant mountains. On hard days it is full of atmosphere with its surrounding dark shapes, restless waters, lashing branches and wild skies. Across the lake is Brandlehow Park, the first piece of land ever purchased by the National Trust of which Canon Rawnsley, to whom Friars Crag is dedicated, was a founding member. Canon Rawnsley who was a great admirer of Ruskin served at the Church of St Kentigern in Crosthwaite, north of Keswick, for 34 years, and during that period he devoted much time and energy to fighting for the preservation of the lakes' scenery and the people's way of life. He loved, and wrote prolifically about both. Lord's Island is also dedicated to Canon Rawnsley, and the National Trust owns St Herbert's Island in the centre of the

lake, the home of the hermit saint who was a friend and disciple of St Cuthbert and whose prayers were answered, Bede tells us, when he and St Cuthbert died on the same day. Friars Crag is so-called because it is reputed to have been an assembly-point for pilgrims visiting the island. In winter sometimes the islands are held in an ice-grip, since this is one of the few shallow lakes, and there is good entertainment to be had for skaters. Canon Rawnsley writing in 1899 remembered, 'the beauty of the scene lay largely in the glorious reflections of the sun-lit snowy hills...one seemed to be skating partly on blue sky, and partly upon the gold-lit mountain peaks of Skiddaw.'

Under the shadow of Skiddaw, and with Grisedale Pike on its western horizon – Norman Nicholson's 'rounded sulky fells of the older slate' – and surrounded by its alluvial plain sits Keswick, 'the source of sandwiches, the guarantee of a dry change and a square meal at evening, headquarters of all delight' according to the mountaineering writer Graham Sutton. Any region with a strong identity built through geographical isolation will have its customs

which are difficult for newcomers to adjust to, and conversely will regard newcomers, however tolerantly, with a degree of caution. Even so, cosmopolitan Keswick from the sixteenth century onwards has absorbed mining engineers from Germany, poets from southern England and their train of Victorian sighteers, mountaineering enthusiasts from England's public schools and office desks, and tourists from local industrial towns and today from all corners of the earth. Some of the town's old and picturesque areas have been flattened to make room, but Keswick in its superlative setting of mountain and lake is still a handsome town. Its name has its origins in yet another activity, since Keswick is currently thought to derive from *Kesevic*, meaning 'cheese farm.' Another theory makes the modern name a corruption of a Norse proper name. Built of local stone and predominantly Victorian, Cumberland's former county capital has for an information centre its pretty, Germanic Moot Hall with tower and spirelet, built in 1813. In its museum among the geological displays and the famous musical stones are memorabilia of nineteenth-century poets and writers, among

them Wordsworth, Robert Southey – an earlier poet laureate – and Coleridge's son, Hartley. Keswick was the home of Coleridge and Southey and, for a time, Percy Bysshe Shelley and his bride, a runaway couple avoiding not the bride's father but the bridegroom's. Unlike Cockermouth, the birthplace of Wordsworth, a more peripheral town with broad tree-lined streets, Keswick's main literary associations are with settlers rather than natives of the area – and indeed Wordsworth was the only major poet of the time born and bred in the region. Before this period, in Elizabeth I's reign, Keswick was a mining centre smelting ore sent from Coniston. Later the town thrived on graphite (plumbago) from the Borrowdale Fells around Seathwaite, which it made into pencils. Pencils are still produced, but the graphite is imported now. The town's main industry is tourism, although it seems to have avoided vulgarisation and makes a grey and respectable backcloth for the ever-increasing crowds of sightseers, motor-boat enthusiasts, cragsmen (hung about with rope), back-packers and culture seekers that throng its narrow streets. Its parish church, dedicated to St

Under the shadow of the mountains, Castlerigg Stone Circle marks time. The Bronze-Age people who erected the circle found the floors and slopes of the valleys too marshy and overgrown, and occupied the tops of the lower fells.

Sailing into the mountains on Ullswater. This narrow, winding lake reaches for about 7 miles from low limestone country on the edge of the National Park to the volcanic rocks of the craggy Helvellyn range.

Kentigern and set apart from the town in Crosthwaite, holds sixteenth-century brasses to Sir John Radcliffe and his wife who owned sizeable estates of rich mining land and whose family formerly built on Lord's Island on Derwent Water. There is a white marble reclining statue of Southey, a regular worshipper, and the church's baptistry commemorates its celebrated incumbent of the last century, Canon Rawnsley. Rebuilt in the fifteenth century and restored in the eighteenth, the church has witnessed the successively-changing fortunes of Keswick and its people played out between the restless waters of the lake and brooding Skiddaw.

Before he lived at Keswick Canon Rawnsley, fresh off the Manchester train and ascending the slopes of Skiddaw, stopped to contemplate the view and to consider the past from the days of St Herbert and his island which he saw 'dark upon the burnished mirror.' Just below '...the wyke, or haven, in which Ketel, the son of Ormr, ran his boats ashore, which gave its name to the town of Ketel's Wyke, or Keswick, as it is pronounced today, was clear to be seen...' Further up, from the site of a Roman camp, the rambler looked down on the 'Druids' Circle' which is now known as Castlerigg Stone Circle, and is one of England's most dramatically-sited and atmospheric standing stone monuments. The stones predate the Druids by nearly 2000 years and it is thought that in common with the others, Castlerigg's stones were set up either as a place of worship or as a natural calendar, or both. The alignment of the circle with its Pennine neighbour Long Meg indicates the direction of the sunrise on May 1. The siting of the circle on a hill overlooking the valley of Naddle Beck achieves its drama through a sense of elevation while Skiddaw and Saddleback rise on the northern skyline.

Just south of Keswick and the stone circle and separated from Derwent Water by Castlerigg Fell is Thirlmere, which Canon Rawnsley called 'the water-ford that gives us men of the thirsty city cool refreshment.' Earlier in 1894, as vicar of Crosthwaite, he had opened the ceremony of 'turning on' the Thirlmere reservoir and earlier still had joined in the fierce battle for the lake's conservation recently described by Molly Lefebure in her book *Cumberland Heritage*. Before the flooding of the valley, there had been two smaller lakes. Now,

...it might be a lake from some other country, or even out of a fairy tale, with its dark pine forests and shadow-filled, silver-streaked expanses of water...the Man-

cunians who promised Lakeland a new Thirlmere more beautiful than the old one had ever been meant every word of what they said and they searched into the backs of their minds for all that a perfectly beautiful lake meant to them and came up with this nurseryland fantasia by Hans Anderson out of the Brothers Grimm...it is never a Cumberland mere.'

The battle for Thirlmere stung the conservationists into forming the National Trust; it was, wrote Molly Lefebure in 1970, 'the greatest and most emotional of all such controversies, until the A66 road battle, now waging.' That battle of a decade ago, from the conservationists' point of view, was lost. The A594 westward from Penrith to Keswick was widened and straightened and called the A66, and now forms a link with the M6. It does much to relieve congestion in the season but, as the National Park Information Service points out in its leaflet *Transport and Communication,* 'the alien effect of straight roads and wide verges will always be there.'

Thirlmere lies to the north of central Lakeland, linked by road to Grasmere across the Dunmail Raise, a route favoured by William and Dorothy Wordsworth. The pass is so-called because it was here that the Anglo-Saxon King Edmund of Northumbria gained Cumbria from the Norse King Dunmail who is said to have fled towards Grisedale Tarn, into which he flung his crown jewels. Another local legend has it that the defeated Norsemen return each year to retrieve their treasure. This ghostly terrain formed part of the Lake District's web of smuggling routes, and carried goods that came from the coast via Wasdale and Watendlath to the head of Thirlmere, over Dunmail Raise and eastward in the defeated King's footsteps past Grisedale Tarn to Patterdale and Ullswater. Ullswater, Patterdale and the third-highest mountain, Helvellyn, provide the classic approach to the lakes from the north east. Like Windermere Ullswater is long and winding, but it lies in a nest of hills whose geology varies and thereby alters the character of the lake as it winds through pretty woodland under the smoother bulkier fells of the Skiddaw slates to the volcanic rocks of central Lakeland, of which Helvellyn is queen. Like Windermere, too, Ullswater provided waterborne delights for Victorian tourists, although the steamers formed part of the region's transport system and were not there solely for pleasure. Today both lakes are public highways which are used for water sports, and can be toured by pleasure boat from end to end. From Pooley Bridge where the lower

limestone country touches the tip of the lake and stretches away to Penrith and the Eden Valley the boat passes well-loved spots that are worthy of exploration on foot, among them Gowbarrow Park where Wordsworth 'wandered lonely as a cloud' and saw his 'host, of golden daffodils.' His sister Dorothy's record of their ramble has a different flavour: 'It was a threatening, misty morning, but mild. We set off after dinner from Eusemere. Mrs Clarkson went a short way with us, but turned back.' The walkers came across the daffodils which 'tossed and reeled and danced,' and on their return 'the landlady looked sour, but it is her way. William was sitting by a good fire when I came downstairs…We had a glass of warm rum and water. We enjoyed ourselves, and wished for Mary.' Gowbarrow which was a medieval deer park, and still supports red deer, can be approached from the A592 leading along the eastward bank of the lake. A short climb passing a folly, Lynulph's Tower, brings you to Aira Force which falls 60 feet down Aira Beck. The name 'Lynulph' is said to derive from L'Ulf, the Norse chieftain after whom Ullswater is named, but Mrs Lynn Linton described the tower as 'a mere modern make-believe, with glazed

windows among the ivy and cucumber frames at the tops of the towers.' Of Aira Force she wrote, 'It is a place where the young would love their hope the best, the mature would cling most proudly to their choice, and the aged dream back over the past and the lost.' Many stretches of this lovely lake are as rewarding: the reaches where you can walk beneath leaves of drooping trees beside the water's edge, or the burnished leaves of autumn seen across the water under the shadowy fells; razor-sharp Striding Edge, reaching from Helvellyn's cloud-cap, held between the green arms of Grisedale and Glenridding whose patchwork pastures stretch to the lake's shore. The bony stretch beneath Striding Edge, as it touches the lake, is clothed in woodland. Grisedale and Glenridding's valleys were scoured by glaciers and the high arêtes of Striding Edge and its neighbour Swirral Edge were honed in the process. The village of Glenridding, Ullswater's southern resort, was until the 1960s a mining settlement whose iron mines were situated above the village, and the miners' tracks now form one of the routes leading toward the summit of Helvellyn, 3118 feet high.

There are several ways up the mountain, none

of them demanding enough for a climber, although there are some crags and gullies that give good sport. One ascent starts from Patterdale, the valley at the head of the lake, and another from Grasmere, while according to Mrs Lynn Linton 'The heroic way from Keswick to Ullswater is straight over Helvellyn.' This is the Lake District's most popular mountain, perhaps because it is so close to beautiful and accessible lakes and is easy to climb, and gives excitement to those with strong heads and footwear who approach by way of Striding Edge. From its seat overshadowing Thirlmere, Helvellyn's ridges radiate to link a series of fells reaching northward as far as Thelkeld and its valley beneath Saddleback, and south to Nethermost Pike and Dollywaggon Pike which rises over Grisedale Tarn. The old pack-horse route to Grasmere starts at Seat Sandal south of the tarn and follows Great Tongue along Tongue Gill as it flows to meet the River Rothay. Helvellyn's slopes plunge steeply to Wythburn and its tiny church, which was threatened with drowning when Thirlmere's valley was flooded, but survives at the lake's head. The eastern arms of Striding Edge and Swirral Edge, reaching less steeply, hold Red Tarn at their

head; this was the scene of a tragedy early last century when the body of the poet Charles Gough was discovered after he had lain dead for three months after a fall, guarded by his dog. A memorial to the dog, put up in 1890, carries lines by Wordsworth and Scott.

As we walk Striding Edge, ramble the bracken and heather slopes of Skiddaw, gape at the cragsmen on Sca Fell or trace the steps of the poets, we pass farmsteads, pastures, and flocks of sheep moving like clouds across the fells: living monuments to all that is beautiful about the lakes. Their stories, too, are recorded, and can be recalled at the scenes of their telling.

Snow-covered Skiddaw towers over Keswick on the northern shores of Derwent Water. The full grandeur of this view takes in Swinside, Lord's Seat, Skiddaw and Skiddaw's 'Laal Man'.

5 Home Ground

The tragedy of Charles Gough and his faithful friend made an impact upon the local shepherds as well as the poets, and Canon Rawnsley recorded a conversation overheard at a shepherds' meet high up on Helvellyn:

'The dog was a fair skeleton hissel' when he was found, and like eneuf poor thing, for he had had nowt but a rabbit or two or a bit of carrion-sheep from one of the ghyll bottoms, you kna, whoal time,' said one.

'Dog was a laal yellow sort of a tarrier,' put in another.

'...Ah, dogs can feel a'most as much as a man,' muttered a shepherd. 'If I speak rough to Vic theer, dog's wasted for a whoal day, it seems to mourn sea.'

The Lake District – Westmorland, Cumberland and North Lancashire – must be one of the best-documented regions in Britain. The lives and language of its people are reflected by the poets and essayists who have lived or settled there, have made it their business to record scenes of country life and have attempted to reproduce the Cumbrian dialect. Much of the writing comes from late last century or the beginning of this one, and since then farming methods have changed as modern techniques have reduced hardship while greater economic pressures are applied to farmers through fierce competition in a world market. The region as a whole has become heavily dependent on dairy farming which is practised in the rich, drier valleys and outlying lowlands while other important traditional industries – textiles, mining, slate quarrying – are reduced or have vanished. Even so the fundamental nature of the lakes' hill farms with their bulky, white-faced Herdwick sheep remains much as it was when the first tourists arrived around 200 years ago.

The fell farmers have left their imprint on the land in the shape of stone farmsteads which follow traditional patterns, and drystone walls that follow the billowy contours. Walling was, and is, a skilled and arduous task. Most of the Lake District's straight walls on the lower lands were built after the Enclosure Acts of the late nineteenth century but some are thought to be ancient structures; perhaps it was the older walls which Hugh Walpole described as 'running like live things about the fells.' Like the farmhouses, most are built of local stone and can be made of limestone, sandstone, granite or slate. Traditionally, farms were let together with their flocks, and included that part of the open fell which the sheep know to be theirs – their 'heaf' – from which they rarely stray, and which usually needs no walls. The walls enclose meadows, or inbye land, close to the farm buildings, where hay is grown and sheep are brought for mating or lambing. Hill cattle spend most of the year here, but the hardy sheep belong on the fell. They are brought down for washing, clipping and branding, and dipping, and in hard weather shepherds climb the fells to dig their flocks out of the snow where sheep can stay alive, buried and without food, for days and even weeks. Writing in the early 1900s William Palmer, a journalist who came of shepherd stock, described the aftermath of a snowstorm:

The dogs were brought out, and, just as the white blast again seethed up the dale, we began to locate the missing animals. The snow was not yet crusted with frost, and at every step we sank deep into the powdery mass; but the collies, though floundering up to the hips at every moment, could still scent the buried sheep. The gale had now become so furious that the topmost layers of snow were being swept down into our excavation almost as fast as our spades could throw them out... the storm seemed more than once likely to add to its prisoners by burying men, dogs, and all in the common heap...

In all such activities the farmer is aided by his dog, which must be as hardy, as skilled and, when necessary, as gentle, as his master. Other native writers have given more light-hearted accounts of traditional tasks like sheep washing, or clipping – which, as this verse from a poem by William Dickinson shows, were high-spirited affairs:

Sek bleatin' o' lambs, and sek barkin' o' dogs,
    Sek jybin and jwokin' o' men;
Sek clatt'rin o'lads in their oald cokert clogs,
    Sek drinkin' o' whisky. Amen!

One place where the lives of the statesmen can be traced is Town End in the village of Troutbeck, a farmhouse formerly occupied by a fell-farming family and now open to the public and in care of the National Trust. Like most buildings of the lakes this one dates from the advent of peace in the seventeenth century, when the abundant and durable local stone began to be used in place of timber, wattle and daub. Originally the house followed the traditional pattern, having the farmworking area at one end and the living quarters at the other, but this became modified over the generations as the occupants grew more prosperous. Inside, the carved oaken furniture

and the possessions that belong to the house give the same sense of solidity and permanence that you can feel if you meet a farmer driving his sheep on a lonely road, or visit one of the towns on a market day. Scattered through their long narrow dales within sight and sound of the splashing becks and under the shadow of the hills, as at Troutbeck, the cottages and farms of the lakes show a variety of styles and moods brought by the different kinds of building stone, a colourwash, or perhaps an adaptation such as the addition of a spinning gallery, dating from the period when farmers' families grew and spun their own wool.

Troutbeck's long valley at its northern end is overlooked by a tongue of land that was farmed by Beatrix Potter after her marriage, and after she had written the books which were to make her famous and which call more visitors to her first farm in Near Sawrey than to any other property in the Lake District, including Wordsworth's Dove Cottage. Some historians argue that Troutbeck Park was crossed by the Romans' High Street, and traces of British settlement have been found. The land is seen most strikingly as the motor road begins to descend from Kirkstone Pass to the

Drystone walls are still built or repaired in the dales and along the roadsides; barbed wire, unsightly but practical, prevents the sheep from jumping over.

valley. Just before it comes into view, before the road has rounded Broad End, another side-road dives westward for Ambleside down a one-in-four descent known as The Struggle. At Ambleside modern roads and pack-horse tracks meet the Roman road linking their fort in Ambleside to the fort on Hardknott Pass which guards the road to Ravenglass. The Romans were 'off-comers' and remained so, but after a visit to the remains of their fort high up at Hardknott Pass it is difficult not to feel admiration at their achievement in building and surviving in these exposed areas, surrounded by desolate mountains, facing the power and waywardness of the weather.

The vagaries of the mountain climate are faced annually by local people and visitors who enact or watch the traditional ceremonies and pastimes that take place, usually in summer. Among the most picturesque, even when it rains and blows, are the rushbearing ceremonies that are celebrated at Ambleside and Grasmere and some of the smaller outlying villages like Musgrave and Urswick. This ancient custom has its origins in pre-Reformation times when churches had earthen floors which at some periods were used for burials, and which were strewn with fresh rushes every year in late summer or early autumn. Today's ceremonies stem from the Victorian era when the poets and their friends began to take an interest, and when the rumbustious celebrations which then accompanied the proceedings were replaced by a more formal programme. The town's brass band leads a procession of children bearing their 'burden,' intricately decorated crosses of rushes and flowers, through the town. In Ambleside the Rushbearing Hymn, which was composed in 1835 by Owen Lloyd who lived there, is sung in the market place:

> Our fathers to the house of God,
> As yet a building rude,
> Bore offerings from the flowery sod
> And fragrant rushes strewed.

After a church service, the children are presented with a piece of gingerbread, and in some villages 'tea is served in the village hall' – a tradition as welcome as it is inextinguishable.

Another tradition which attracts holidaymakers takes the form of the Grasmere Sports held in the natural amphitheatre of valley and encircling hills. Canon Rawnsley in 1899 remembered a time when 'chairs and forms were brought out of the nearest cottages for the few ladies and gentlemen to sit on'; things had changed by the

Fertile pasture under the fells: farmland in Troutbeck, man's contribution to nature's beauty.

57

Where the mountains come down to the sea. The Cumbrian coast at Ravenglass which was once the main port of the north-west, and is thought to contain stone from the Roman site at Glannaventa nearby.

time of his writing and today a crowd of thousands gathers to watch. Originally the spectators and participants would have consisted of shepherds, woodsmen, mill workers or miners and quarrymen from all parts of Westmorland, Cumberland and North Lancashire. Part of the attraction of the games at Grasmere and lesser-known centres stems from the important rôle played by the terrain in events like the Senior 'Guides' Races' to the top of the nearest fell and back, an event that has undergone profound changes since Canon Rawnsley's time when the race was undertaken not, as today, by professional sportsmen, but by shepherds and farmers: 'Watch him through the field-glasses; the way in which he throws himself rather than leaps down, his hands often above his head as he steadies himself in the downward plunge, fairly startles one.' The race is completed within 15 minutes, though the August rain often makes the going harder. Rain makes little impression on the dedicated sports followers, so caught up are they in pole jumping, high leaping, leap frogging, hound trailing and – perhaps best of all – that most benign and skilled of sports, Cumberland or Westmorland wrestling. Among the older events that take place in Cumbria's summer programme, the Egremont Crab Fair has been held continuously in times of peace since 1267, and has attractions like the greasy pole where instead of the more picturesque sheep's carcase of former days a pound note awaits the winner at the top of the pole 30 feet above ground and gives proof that it is the glory which counts and not the prize. More recent additions to the season are Kendal's Folk and Jazz Festivals and an exhibition by the Guild of Lakeland Craftsmen which shows work and skills ranging from carved walking sticks to glass-blowing.

Writing in 1940, Norman Nicholson mentioned 'folk dances and ceremonies which are preserved with desperate enthusiasm in the way that ornithologists protect a bird that is nearly extinct' and no-one in those days could have foreseen the upsurge in interest that has revived traditional skills, dances and songs. Today's versions may be more for spectators than were their originals, but they are welcomed by many as alternatives to the canned entertainments of the twentieth century. The survival of other Cumbrian traditions has no need of the enthusiasm of conservationists because, as Norman Nicholson pointed out over 40 years ago, the traditions are still 'a vital part of the life of

58

the people, and no more need to be preserved than love-making.' Of these, sheep dog trials, hound trailing and fox hunting predominate, and the trials perhaps show most satisfyingly (and comfortably) the fell farmer's close contact with the living materials on which he builds his own life – his dogs and his sheep. Wordsworth noted it:

Waving his hat, the shepherd, from the vale,
Directs his winding dog the cliffs to scale;
The dog, loud barking, 'mid the glittering rocks,
Hunts, where his master points, the intercepted flocks.

The trials are not held on the difficult terrain of some fell pastures, but they require all the skills to be performed in a formalised setting under public scrutiny, and using sheep unknown to the dog and his master, which is possibly even harder. The five sheep, sometimes at first out of sight of the shepherd, are 'gathered' by the dog, then guided through a series of hurdles as the dog obeys varying hand or whistle signals, and then – with the aid of the handler – are penned. The three sections have to be accomplished within a certain time, but this is small hardship in a task which often faces cruel and unpredictable weather conditions where time can be of the essence. Points are awarded for successful completion of each of the three sections, and for style.

Sheep dog trials and hound trailing were given the stamp of official approval near the turn of the century. The Hound Trailing Association was formed in 1906, and the sport has come to have special interest for the mining fraternity, perhaps because it is usually more pleasantly-sited, but makes an equally exciting alternative to greyhound racing. A trail of paraffin and aniseed is laid over fell and down dale; the hounds are slipped and run the trail with watchers occupying fixed vantage points rather than following on foot, as they do in the unpredictable and more functional fox hunt. Unlike the sheep dog trials both pastimes make use of the countryside, but in one all that you are likely to lose is your bet, while in fox hunting animals' lives and humans' livelihoods are at stake. Fox hunting is a mixture of business and pleasure whose season lasts from autumn to spring, although the hounds may be called out at any time of the year if a fox has been harrying lambs or snatching poultry. Perhaps the best-known fell pack is the Blencathra, known as much on its own merits as from its lineage which included at least one of John Peel's Caldbeck pack given to his friend John Crozier after Peel's

death in 1854. The Caldbeck hounds' blood could be traced in the Blencathra pack at least until 1900. Caldbeck is an outlying village north-east of the Skiddaw block, more of Cumberland than of Lakeland, while Blencathra takes its title from the Celtic name for the lakes' Saddleback. Fox and hounds observe no such distinctions and go where they will, often covering many miles of mountain and valley, cliff and scree and bog, from one end of the region to another and beyond. The chase is gruelling and can be followed in the dales by car or on horseback, although for spectators it is often better to remain on foot and keep to the fell tops, as this gives a better overall vantage-point. Those taking active part dismount and follow on foot as the fox climbs ever higher in his efforts to escape the hounds at his heels. Only those who are at home on the fells in all weathers can take part easily. Bolt-holes are covered before the start, which in winter can be before dawn, and any cranny the fox does find – often in an almost impossibly inaccessible position – may have to be unblocked with a crowbar or spade to send the terrier down.

This cruel spectacle is not really a sport, and as a ritual it has its roots in the primitive rivalry between man and fox for the lives of the sheep upon which both depend. It has always been true that a farmer must have his heart as well as his mind set upon his job, and so it is that the rivalry can become an obsession. The hunt goes out two or three times a week in season, and the Blencathra pack covers a wide ground including Skiddaw and Saddleback. John Peel's friend John Crozier rests in Threlkeld churchyard after 64 years as Master of the Hunt, and like Peel he is commemorated in verse:

The hunt is up, the hunt is up;
Auld Tolly's in the drag;
Hark to him, beauties, git away,
He's gone for Skiddaw Crag.
Rise fra ye'r beds, ye sleepy-heads,
If ye wad plesser know;
Ye'r hearts 't will cheer, if ye bit hear
John Crozier's 'Tally-ho!'

Caldbeck churchyard holds the beautiful headstone of John Peel which appropriately is decorated with relief carvings of hound and horn, the rising sun, vine leaves and grapes. Peel was a fell farmer who like many others achieved a local reputation as a hard-drinking and brilliant Master of the Pack, and whose name is universally known through the song written by a friend, John

Gentle outlying pastures at the foot of Wast Water obscure the lake in its bleak setting beneath the distant Wasdale Hills.

Woodcock Graves, as they sat companionably in front of a fire after a day following the hounds. The song, which was set to a traditional ballad, did not become an all-time hit until it was given a rousing new tune by William Metcalfe, conductor of the Carlisle Church Music Society, some years after Peel's death. The words say little of the character of the man, nor need they, for he belonged to a breed that was well-known. Here he is described by John Graves: 'he was of a very limited education beyond hunting, but no wile of fox or hare could elude his scrutiny; business of any shape was utterly neglected, often to cost beyond the first loss.' Others remembered his 'lang lappeted cwoat of hodden-grey homespun and leather knee-brutches and ankle jacks, and a tall boxer hat,' and his 'fine gert neb and grey eyes that could see for iver.' His pack is best recalled in Graves's song:

Yes, I kenn'd John Peel, an aul Ruby too,
Ranter and Royal and Bellman as true;
Fra the drag to the chase, an' the chase to the view,
An' the view to the deeth in the mwornin.'

Apart from its hunting associations Caldbeck still has relics of the mills that were engaged in bobbin-making or in the production of cloth that made John Peel's 'cwoat seay gray,' and to which the village owed its existence. Built in the 1830s, the Lakeland bobbin mills by their rushing streams have closed, although you can see one by Stock Ghyll near Ambleside and visit the working museum at Stott Park, while mills remain working at Staveley and at Spark Bridge, which got its name from the iron industry in the eighteenth century. Wood for iron smelting, as far back as the fifteenth or sixteenth centuries, was indiscriminately cut and used in 'bloomeries,' or hearths cut into the ground along the lakeside where iron ore was heated between layers of wood and charcoal from which the carbon reacted with the ore to produce workable iron. On the banks of Coniston Water and Windermere, closest to the Furness area which was the centre of the early iron industry, remains of the bloomeries are still visible. In the nineteenth century wood for smelting was produced by 'coppicing' – cutting oak, ash or hazel trees at the base every 12 to 15 years, to induce growth of long, straight poles. This gave rise to a number of trades or crafts like besom, barrel or swill-basket making. Now only the beautiful coppice woods remain, most striking at places like Elter Water, the Norsemen's *Eltrvatr*,

'Lake of the Swans,' or on the road between Hawkshead and Newby Bridge.

Another grave at Caldbeck commemorates a figure that achieved renown quite innocently at the hands of an imposter then calling himself the Hon. Alexander Augustus Hope who, a middle-aged man and leaving a trail of broken women and bad debts, married Mary Robinson, the 25-year-old daughter of the proprietor of the Fish Inn, Buttermere. Unfortunately for John Hatfield the trail ended there for he was recognised, tried for forgery and hanged within a year of his bigamous marriage. His bride, 'The Beauty of Buttermere,' had been locally known before her marriage, since in 1792 at the age of 15 she had been noted as a country lovely by one of the early guide writers, Captain Joseph Budworth. Now she became nationally known, the subject of romances and melodramas, and for some years the Fish Inn had something beyond the boating and angling, 'most charming Scenery and pure air', to rival its neighbours. Mary, whose family were Cumberland statesman stock, married a Caldbeck farmer and brought up a family there, and thus made the choice that so many would envy – to reject the glamour of the cities and to rejoin the farming community whose culture belongs to the lakes' truest and most ancient heritage.

Mary's story seems almost a parallel of the lakes' story of the last two centuries. Britain's biggest beauty spot, it has achieved renown for its untouched scenery and thereby has attracted the attention of millions who have wandered, rambled, climbed and eulogised. While the cities have flooded its farmland for water, the Forestry Commission has planted its slopes with sombre conifers. It is said that to measure a thing is to change it, and thus 'measured' by visitors and others the Lake District has changed. Other rural areas of great beauty in Britain have undergone similar changes which today are seen as part of the overall shift away from traditional industries, the amazing technological advances in communications, and the increased leisure-time demands of city dwellers. The dangers of over-popularity have been recognised in the Lake District, which is protected by its status as a National Park and by the activities of the National Trust. The former has sponsored a scheme for reviving traditional industries by setting up craftshops at Coniston, a village which has retained its quarrying industry, while the latter through guardianship of hill farms has

Sizergh Castle, built as a peel tower in the 1340s and extended over later centuries. Its 1556 acres contain lakes, rivers, waterfalls, rock gardens and a collection of rare ferns.

maintained Lakeland's rural character and preserved the human touch that makes pleasant harmony with this landscape of lakes lying in the laps of their ancient mountains. It is this harmony which perhaps brings most pleasure to we who visit this lovely place, and whether our appreciation and that of the lakes' native population is expressed in poetry, in repeated return visits, in the satisfaction felt by a farmer carrying out seasonal duties that have occupied his forbears for generations, or in the games and sports and celebrations that make a counterpoint to a demanding occupation, the common desire surely must be for the preservation of the lakes' singular beauties and the continuation without hardship of the lakes' dwellers' traditional industries and pastimes.

Hadrian's Wall extending eastward from Cuddy's Crag toward the Roman fort of Housesteads. This section is one of the most dramatic of the 75-mile wall now surviving.